The House Was Filled with the Fragrance of the Perfume

Cardinal Fernando Filoni

The House Was Filled with the Fragrance of the Perfume

A Spirituality of the Order of the Holy Sepulchre

EWTN PUBLISHING, INC.
Irondale, Alabama

EWTN Publishing, Inc.
5817 Old Leeds Road, Irondale, AL 35210

Distributed by Sophia Institute Press, Box 5284, Manchester, NH 03108.

paperback ISBN 978-1-68278-234-7

ebook ISBN 978-1-68278-235-4

LCCN: 2021936825

First printing

Contents

The House Was Filled with the Fragrance of the Perfume

Introduction

Members of the Order of the Holy Sepulchre of Jerusalem often pose the question as to whether membership in this ancient and noble institution entails its own "spirituality." This is a pertinent question given that it is not simply an honorific chivalric Order. Rather, it is a vital and active body with responsibilities and commitments that have been gradually entrusted to it by the Pontiffs who reorganized it. Indeed, beginning with Pope Pius IX (in 1847 and 1868) and then his successors, the Popes over the centuries further modified and modernized it.[1] Moreover,

---

[1] Of ancient origin, it was further reorganized, enlarged, and enriched with responsibilities and privileges also by the Supreme Pontiffs Leo XIII (1888), Pius X (1907, who reserved the title of Grand Master to

the very Constitution requires that Members practice the Gospel virtues.[2] This is the reason I will offer further reflection on some of the more significant elements of the spirituality of the Order, identifying its roots, but not without responding first to the question: Who are its Members?

First, it must be said that the Apostolic See recognizes and confers various chivalric orders and

---

the Pope himself), Pius XI, Pius XII (1940, who gave the Order a cardinal as Grand Master in 1949), John XXIII (1962), Paul VI (1977), and John Paul II (1994, who established the Blessed Virgin Mary, Queen of Palestine, as Patron). The age-old and benevolent concern of the Popes for the inhabitants of the Holy Land grew during and after the various wars of the twentieth century in Palestine; this partly explains the opportunity, in the *mens* of the Pontiffs, to alleviate the suffering of the people residing there, regardless of political or religious affiliations. See Benedict XV, Allocutions *Antequam Ordinem* (1919), in *AAS* 11, pp. 99–101; *Nobis Quidem* (1921), in *AAS* 11, p. 259; Pius XI, *Gratum Nobis* (1923), in *AAS* 15, pp. 249–252; Apostolic Constitution *Servatoris Jesu Christi* (1925), in *AAS* 17, p. 612.

2   Constitution approved by Pope Francis, May 11, 2020, art. 1.

honorific titles.[3] Speaking specifically about the Equestrian Order of the Holy Sepulchre of Jerusalem, it is affirmed that the institution is "under the protection of the Holy See" (*subcollazione pontificia*), as if to underline the juridical status that is not merely honorific.[4] At the head of the Order is the Grand Master, who is appointed by the Supreme Pontiff, aided by the Grand Magisterium. Laity are admitted, men and women, in this case as Knights and Dames, who demonstrate their desire to become Members. It is also open to clergy (bishops, priests, and deacons) especially clerics committed to fostering the

[3] *Annuario Pontificio* 2020 lists the following: the Supreme Order of Christ, the Order of the Golden Spur, the Pian Order, the Order of Saint Gregory the Great, and the Order of Saint Sylvester, Pope and Martyr. There are also mentions of two distinctions: the *Pro Ecclesia et Pontifice* Cross and the *Benemerenti* Medal.

[4] In the Constitution, it is stated that, "Because of its activity, the Order acts as a Central Entity of the Catholic Church, in accordance with article 11 of the Lateran Treaty dated 11 February 1929" (art. 2 § 1); furthermore, that, "due to its nature and its strictly religious and charitable purposes, is extraneous to any movement or stances of a political character" (art. 2 § 3).

spiritual progress and growth of all the Members.[5] The specific mission assigned to the Order by the Holy Father is to have the ecclesial community at heart and to nourish zeal toward the Land of Christ in order to support the Catholic Church and the Christian presence there.[6]

So what does having a spirituality actually mean? What life projects, convictions, value systems, and choices are proper to a Knight or Dame of the Equestrian Order of the Holy Sepulchre of Jerusalem? Before delving into the subject, which will draw on relevant biblical and ecclesiological dimensions, it is appropriate to note that it is the Order itself that gives primary importance to the vocation to holiness of its Members and aspires to be an instrument of development and of deepening the spiritual progress of each and every person in the environment in which they live and practice their Faith.

As Pope Francis underlines to Members of the Consulta:

[5] See Constitution, Preamble.
[6] See Constitution, art. 1.

Certainly, the continuous growth of the Order depends on your unceasing and ever renewed effort. In this regard, it is important not to forget that the principal aim of your Order lies in the spiritual growth of its members. Therefore, any success of your initiatives cannot be separate from appropriate religious formation programmes addressed to every Knight and every Dame, so that they may consolidate their own indispensable relationship with the Lord Jesus, especially in prayer, in meditation on the Sacred Scriptures and in furthering their knowledge of the doctrine of the Church. It is a task, especially for you leaders, to offer the example of an intense spiritual life and true following of the Lord: in this way you can render a valid service of authority to those under your leadership.[7]

---

[7] Francis, Address to the Members of the Consulta of the Equestrian Order of the Holy Sepulchre of Jerusalem, (November 16, 2018). It should be emphasized that if there were no sharing of love for the Holy Land, together with a spirituality founded on the mystery of the suffering, death, and Resurrection

For bishops, priests, and deacons, spirituality is intimately connected to their vocation as men of God, friends of the Bridegroom,[8] united to Him with participation in the triple office of Christ: teacher, priest, and king. Their lives must therefore tend and adapt to the teaching of Jesus: "Be perfect, therefore, as your heavenly Father is perfect."[9] In the previously mentioned address, Pope Francis recalled that

> admission ... of Bishops, Priests and Deacons is not entirely an honour. It is part of their duties of pastoral service to assist those among you who have a role of responsibility by providing

---

of Christ, the root of belonging and service to the Order would disappear. The Consulta is an advisory body of the Grand Magisterium for the most important issues.

[8] According to the convincing expression of St. John Paul II: "The Church, as the spouse of Jesus Christ, wishes to be loved by the priest in the total and exclusive manner in which Jesus Christ her head and spouse loved her." Post-Synodal Apostolic Exhortation *Pastores Dabo Vobis* (March 25, 1992), no. 29.

[9] Matt. 5:48, NIV. For reference, see the Second Vatican Council's teaching in *Presbyterorum Ordinis* (December 7, 1965).

opportunities for community and liturgical prayer at every level, continuous spiritual opportunities, and catechesis for ongoing formation and for the growth of all members of the Order.[10]

The Second Vatican Council recommends to the laity, as part of the Holy People of God and one body[11] together with the clergy and the consecrated, that their foundations rest in Christ and their vital union with Him, as the Lord said: "If you remain in me and I in you, you will bear much fruit; apart from me you can do nothing."[12] It is, however, a union that must be consolidated with a liturgical-sacramental life and that tends to find fertile soil in the ordinary conditions of life through the exercise of faith, hope, and charity and in the light of the Cross and Resurrection of the Lord. It is a union that encourages us to face every aspect of existence with confidence: married

---

[10] Francis, Address to the Members of the Consulta.

[11] Decree on the Apostolate of the Laity *Apostolicam Actuositatem* (AA) (November 18, 1965), no. 18.

[12] John 15:5, NIV.

life, family life, widowhood, celibacy, work, infirmity, social and professional life.[13]

Before proceeding further, it would be worthwhile to recall some typical characteristics of a chivalric order. Obviously, this is not to dwell on a matter that has already been explored in various texts over time, but simply to highlight some significant aspects of valuable knowledge. It is well known that in times past, chivalry was perceived as an organization of self-discipline, rich in generosity and courage, and of virtues that lead to highly ethical behavior on the part of those who belonged to it. Among these lofty virtues we find the most essential the supreme reference to God (*religiositas*,[14]

---

[13] See the aforementioned conciliar decree *Apostolicam Actuositatem* and the Post-Synodal Apostolic Exhortation *Christifideles Laici* (December 30, 1988). The Council had expressed itself favorably with regard to the institutions that, with their aims, contribute to the good of the Church and promote the apostolate and collaboration (see AA 18).

[14] *Religiositas*, the most important of the moral virtues according to St. Thomas Aquinas, consists in rendering to God, with heart and action, the liturgical-sacramental worship due to Him. See *Summa Theologica* (*ST*) II-II, q. 81, art. 6, a. 7; q. 84, art. 9ff.). Moreover, for the Dame and the Knight, the Investiture and the

pietas[15]), prudence (*prudentia*[16]), loyalty (*fides*), faithfulness (*fidelitas*), solidarity among Members (*concordia*), honor and nobility of mind (*dignitas*), an irreproachable civic conduct (*status*), self-abnegation and prowess (*virtus*), gratitude (*gratitudo*), and dedication to loved ones (*amor*). These virtues were held in alternating consideration from their institution in the medieval

---

solemnization of their promise imply the entry into a new dimension of the duty of worship, with new forms of *latria* that are added to those already promised by the original words of the godfather and godmother during Baptism. In its effects, the promise made before the minister of the Church creates new obligations for the Dame and the Knight, as set out in the Constitution of the Order.

[15] In the thought of Thomas Aquinas, with *pietas*, understood as a gift of the Holy Spirit, one turns to God, while with that understood as a human virtue, one turns to one's neighbour (see *ST* II-II, q. 121; q. 101.) Far from scholastic distinctions, for Francis of Assisi, the proto-custodian of the Holy Land, *pietas* lies in the primacy that leads to love one's neighbor with a view to bringing him closer and involving him in this love for the Creator (see *Expositio in Pater Noster* 5).

[16] Each Dame and Knight who has been entrusted with an office of service to other Members of the Order is expected to lead with high virtues in view of the common good of all during her or his temporal mandate.

period until their decline.[17] Despite this, there has been no shortage of Members who, in the practice of these virtues, also made their way to more strikingly religious institutions with the additional vows of chastity, obedience, and poverty.[18]

A prominent figure, who passed from a military institution to the service of the Kingdom of Heaven was Ignatius of Loyola (1491–1556). Borrowing some aspects of chivalry, he founded the Company of Jesus (*Societas Iesu*)[19] and analogized some ideas of the chivalric life, elevating human virtues to Christian and religious virtues. Having experienced a crisis and reflecting on his own chivalric condition—compromised by the

---

[17] In the fifteenth and sixteenth centuries, with the improvement and spread of firearms, chivalry began to decline along with some of the ideals that accompanied it.

[18] See P. Pozzessere, *Ordini Monastico-militari in Occidente* (*secoli XII–XIV*) (2013), ebook. Consider the influence of the Dominicans, founded by St. Dominic de Guzmán (1170–1221); the Franciscans, founded by St. Francis of Assisi (1181–1226); the Carmelites, founded in 1207 by some hermits to whom the Patriarch of Jerusalem gave a rule; and the Augustinian hermits (1256).

[19] The title "company" derives from the founder's military genius in desiring an order for his religious institution as regular clerics.

serious injuries sustained in the defense of Pamplona, in Navarre, Spain, against the French—he decided[20] that his ideals could be better spent for God and for the Church, even more so in the immensely difficult time of the dramatic Protestant schism.[21] Ignatius then imagined[22] himself as a pilgrim to Jerusalem:

[20] In his *metanoia* from worldly knight to pilgrim of Christ in the world, the young Ignatius was inspired by the lives of the saints reported in the *Golden Legend* of the Blessed Archbishop Jacobus de Voragine (Varazze).

[21] While Protestantism under Luther accused Rome of being unfaithful to the Gospel (see A. Pellicciari, *Martin Lutero: il lato oscuro di un rivoluzionario* [Siena: Cantagalli, 2016]), Ignatius put himself at the service of the Gospel, but in fidelity to the Pope, going beyond the human deficiencies of the period. The Company of Jesus then became the most effective instrument of renewal in the Catholic Reformation. See H. Jedin, *Ignatius of Loyola and His Order until 1556*, in *History of the Church*, ed. H. Jedin, vol. 6 (Milan: Jaca Book, 2007), pp. 535ff.

[22] "Having been a passionate devourer of novels and other imaginative books on the amazing feats of famous people, when he began to feel on the mend, Ignatius asked that some be given to him to pass the time. But in the house, where he was hospitalized, no such book was found, so he was given two entitled *Life of Christ* and *Anthology of the Saints*.... He began to read them, and

barefoot, penitent, feeding on herbs, withstanding trials, as many holy pilgrims had done in the past. In thinking about this, he felt intimate consolation and great spiritual joy.[23] He was, in fact, a pilgrim to the Holy Land, where he intended to settle, but his plan did not come to fruition. Providence had other plans for him.

---

as he assimilated their content, he felt a certain interest in the topics that were dealt with.... As he read the life of Christ our Lord and of the saints, he thought to himself ... 'And if I too did what St. Francis did; and if I too imitated the example of St. Dominic?'.... When he thought about the things of the world, he was taken with great pleasure; then, immediately afterward, when suddenly tired, he abandoned them, and found himself sad and withered. Instead, when he imagined that he had to share the austerities he had seen put into practice by the saints, then not only did he feel pleasure while he thought about it, but the joy continued even after." From the *Acts*, collected by Ludovico Consalvo from the mouth of St. Ignatius, chaps. 1, 5–8, *Acta Sanctorum* 7 (July 1868): 647. Translated from the Italian.

[23] With the papal bull *Regimini Militantis Ecclesiae* (September 27, 1540), Pope Paul III confirmed the Society of Jesus, which began with six companions on August 15, 1534, in Montmartre, near Paris. Paul III was severely attacked by Luther. See Pellicciari, *Martin Lutero*, p. 129.

The Biblical Dimension of Spirituality

Jerusalem: The Mystery, Places, and People

In Bethany: A Gesture for Always

Six days before the Jewish Passover, we find Jesus in Bethany, a village not far from Jerusalem, in the house of Lazarus, Martha, and Mary. These friends offered Him a dinner. Lazarus was alive again. After an illness had dragged him into death and after he had been buried for four days, Lazarus had been brought back to life by Jesus. While at dinner,

> Mary took a pound of costly ointment of pure nard and anointed the feet of Jesus and wiped his feet with her hair; and the house was filled with the fragrance of the ointment. But Judas

Iscariot, one of his disciples (he who was to betray him), said, "Why was this ointment not sold for three hundred denarii and given to the poor?" This he said, not that he cared for the poor but because he was a thief, and as he had the money box he used to take what was put into it. Jesus said, "Let her alone, let her keep it for the day of my burial."[1]

Jesus is looking beyond that moment. Mary of Bethany will no longer have the opportunity to show her affection for the Master, and the Master accepts that gesture for the day of His burial. In fact, the Resurrection will anticipate every other gesture of the women who, after the Jewish Passover, would go to complete the anointing of the body of the Lord.

Adherence to the Order allows us to continue the same work of Mary of Bethany — that is, for us also to anoint the Body of Christ, which is the Church, in which Jesus now lives. I refer to the Church in its universal and local reality, but in particular as Members of the Order, to the Mother Church of all the

[1] John 12:3–7.

churches, that of Jerusalem with its faithful, pilgrims, refugees, and poor whom Jesus left to us — "The poor you always have with you, but you do not always have me"[2] — in order to contribute in some way to the good and the religious and social peace that is so necessary in the Holy Land. Every Dame and every Knight, therefore, continues the same work of Mary of Bethany, taking to heart the Person of Jesus living in the Church. Knowing this Body of the Lord and taking care of it in its Members is the high privilege assumed by us in the Equestrian Order of the Holy Sepulchre of Jerusalem.

In truth, now more than ever, we need to care for this Body of Christ, wounded today by incalculable violence, all the more painful when it occurs at the hands of those who were once part of it. Twisted and moralistic reasoning has no place, just as Jesus immediately dismissed Judas' hypocritical reasoning. It is fundamental for a Dame and a Knight to understand that the Church in the world, as desired and understood by Christ and left to us by the apostles, is authentic as "a sacrament or as a sign and instrument

[2] John 12:8.

both of a very closely knit union with God and of the unity of the whole human race."[3]

The sacramentality of the Church touches its most intimate and profound nature, that is, the awareness that it has of itself, infused by Christ, which makes it not a mere human organization, but a gift of God for mankind with a spiritual and moral mission. At the same time, so that it is an instrument of peace and union between peoples, it is devoid of ideological, political, or military calculations. Therefore, being in the Church means participating in the mission of salvation entrusted to it by Jesus while, at the same time, being at the service of men and women, all the more in times of anxiety, social changes, and imbalances that often violate dignity, freedom, and the human person itself.

The Cross and Death of Christ

The powerful symbol of the faith of every Christian, at all times, is the Cross. In it one can see the atrocious

---

[3] Second Vatican Council, Dogmatic Constitution on the Church *Lumen Gentium* (*LG*) (November 21, 1964), no. 1.

mystery of the death of Jesus, with His wounds never healed and yet glorious: almost indelible tattoos, through which Christ, in the act of showing them to the Father, cries and intercedes to obtain mercy for His brothers and sisters because, "they know not what they do."[4] Pope Benedict XVI commented that "at the foot of the Cross, the Church of the Gentiles comes into being," adding that, "through the Cross, the Lord gathers people together to form the new community of the worldwide Church. Through the suffering Son they recognize the true God."[5] It is interesting to note that the death sentence for blasphemy decided by the Sanhedrin[6] did not call for

---

[4] Luke 23:34.

[5] Joseph Ratzinger (Benedict XVI), *Jesus of Nazareth: From the Entrance into Jerusalem to the Resurrection* (San Francisco: Ignatius Press, 2011), p. 224.

[6] "Again the high priest asked him, 'Are you the Christ, the Son of the Blessed?' And Jesus said, 'I am; and you will see the Son of man sitting at the right hand of Power, and coming with the clouds of heaven.' And the high priest tore his mantle, and said, 'Why do we still need witnesses? You have heard his blasphemy. What is your decision?' And they all condemned him as deserving death" (Mark 14:61–64).

crucifixion but for stoning.[7] Death by crucifixion was a Roman penalty.[8] Therefore, a Roman, non-Jewish punishment was requested for Jesus, although it had also entered into the Jewish custom a few years earlier.[9] Crucifixion was considered, in itself, a penalty for slaves and for the most serious crimes.[10] However, [crucifixion] was asked of the Roman procurator for Jesus for [His] having proclaimed Himself to be "King of the Jews." Therefore, it was a request with political motivation: "And Pilate asked him, 'Are you the King of the Jews?'" Although he knew that the alleged charge was untrue and that Jesus had been handed

---

[7] Stephen was stoned to death for blasphemy. See Acts 7:55–60.

[8] See G. Ricciotti, *Vita di Gesù Cristo*, ed. Arnoldo Mondadori (1952), p. 676.

[9] Crucifixion seems to have been introduced by Pompey the Great in 63 B.C. when he took Jerusalem. Cicero had defined crucifixion as the "cruelest and grimmest of punishments." *Against Verres* II, 5, 62–67.

[10] At the end of the Third Servile War, in 71 B.C., crucifixion was the penalty reserved for the slaves who survived the military clash with Crassus and Pompey.

over to him "out of envy,"[11] Pilate allowed him to be crucified with the *titulus* "The King of the Jews."[12]

The punishment inflicted on Jesus contains in itself two complementary aspects. First, there is the condemnation, the work of the Sanhedrin and therefore coming from the Jewish religious sphere. This happened — according to the "prophecy" of Caiaphas, high priest that year — in order to "gather into one the children of God who are scattered abroad."[13] Then comes the death by crucifixion, in the style of punishment inflicted by the pagans; in this way, the universal work of salvation, which comes from the Jews[14] but is destined to illuminate all mankind, was fulfilled.[15]

The Crucifixion of Jesus, His death, took place just outside the walls, in the northern part of Jerusalem. It was a place near a city gate, in an evident position and

[11] Mark 15:2, 10.

[12] Mark 15:26.

[13] John 11:47–53.

[14] See John 4:22.

[15] "The true light that enlightens every man was coming into the world....He came to his own home, and his own people received him not. But to all who received him, who believed in his name, he gave power to become children of God" (John 1:9–12).

on a rocky outcrop colorfully called "the skull,"[16] to serve as a common warning. Close at hand there was a garden where a tomb had been hewn out of rock. The sites of the Crucifixion and burial of our Lord were therefore close to each other. In the fourth century these sites were enclosed within the Constantinian basilica, which would contain within the most sacred space for Christians in Jerusalem.

Therefore, the symbol of the Cross can never appear or be a mere decoration of elegance or distinction.[17] The Cross is the drama of an ignominious and unjust death before men, but voluntarily accepted by Christ. "And by that will we have been sanctified through the offering of the body of Jesus Christ once for all,"[18] comments the author of the Letter to

---

[16] *Calvaria* in Latin; *Golgota* in Aramaic; *Gulgoleth* in Hebrew.

[17] For the Order of the Holy Sepulchre, the Cross—in the form known as the *hierosolimitana*, enhanced by the addition of four minor crosses inserted in the four corners, all red—is the emblem that distinguishes it.

[18] Heb. 10:10; the entire initial passage of chapter 10 of the Letter to the Hebrews explains the theology of Christ's sacrificial offering to the Father for human redemption; see also 1 Cor. 1:18–19.

the Hebrews, according to which it is Jesus Himself Who reveals the meaning of the offering of Himself by appealing to a dialogue between Him and the Father before entering this world: "Consequently, when Christ came into the world, he said, 'Sacrifices and offerings thou hast not desired, but a body hast thou prepared for me; in burnt offerings and sin offerings thou hast taken no pleasure. Then I said, 'Lo, I have come to do thy will, O God.'"[19]

It is therefore from the content of that dialogue that we understand the true meaning of the mystery of the death of Christ, and this helps us to change completely our sacrificial-moralistic idea and to understand the death of Jesus as an act of reconciliation and salvation. The apostle Paul understood this well and wore it as a title of glory before his critics: "But far be it from me to glory except in the cross of our Lord Jesus Christ, by which the world has been crucified to me, and I to the world."[20]

---

[19] Heb. 10:5–7.
[20] Gal. 6:14.

The words of the prophet Zechariah were fulfilled; in a shining vision, he had said: "And I will pour out … a spirit of compassion and supplication…. They look on him whom they have pierced."[21]

The Characters

In the drama of Jesus (His Passion and death), we encounter in the crowd a multitude of faces that give us a glimpse into a society actively against Christ. It is a society that is both intriguing and perverse: inept civil and military authorities (the Roman procurator, the tetrarch);[22] clever and perverted men of the Sanhedrin who condemn and control the execution of the death sentence; priests of the Temple who mock Him; soldiers led by a centurion who rigidly carry out orders; evildoers and a baying crowd. Yet there is also a pious humanity that follows in the footsteps of the Lord: anonymous daughters

---

[21] Zech. 12:10; see parallels with John 3:14; 19:37, Rev. 1:7; Amos 8:10.

[22] Pilate, procurator of the Roman Empire, and Herod Antipas, an Edomite-Palestinian, client of Rome.

of Jerusalem;[23] a farmer, Simon of Cyrene forced to carry the Cross with Him;[24] a mother, Mary, deeply tested and heartbroken by the suffering and death of her Son; the disciple, the one whom Jesus loved;[25] courageous women: Mary the wife of Clopas; Mary Magdalene;[26] Mary, mother of James the lesser and of Joseph; and Salome.[27] Perhaps, near the Cross, there were also other frightened and stunned followers of Jesus, and two wealthy men who went to great pains to retrieve and bury the body of the Lord: Joseph of Arimathea, a member of the Sanhedrin, a good and just man,[28] and Nicodemus, a notable chief of the Jews, and also an admirer of the Master, who had tried to defend Him against the Pharisees.[29] All of these are part of the same humanity that is called to testify for Christ or against Christ, to consider Him an evildoer, an impostor, and a blasphemer or a just

[23] See Luke 23:28.
[24] See Matt. 27:32; Mark 15:21; Luke 23:26.
[25] See John 19:26.
[26] See John 19:25–26.
[27] See Mark 15:40; Matt. 27:55–56.
[28] See Luke 23:50; Mark 15:43.
[29] See John 3:1; 7:51–52.

man, the One Who, in the supreme act of His life, reconciles humanity to God.

Here, further reflection is required, so that it escapes no one that the condemnation of a just man, as recognized by Pilate ("Behold ... I find no crime in him"), as well as by one of the criminals crucified next to Christ ("But this man has done nothing wrong") and even the centurion ("Certainly, this man was innocent"),[30] questions all humanity, yesterday and today. Faced with the mystery of the Cross, everyone remains equally judged. We are faced with the existentially greatest and ontologically deepest mystery—that is, death, and something, moreover, inflicted unjustly and not by mistake.

In the last cry Jesus utters in His life, what comes to mind is not the joyful and surprising first wail of a newborn—two sounds that enclose life—but rather drama, pain, and spasmodic agony. It was a final, excruciating cry that resounded throughout the earth and will continue to do so until the last day—a cry that was a prayer, an entrustment, a plea.

[30] John 19:4; Luke 23:41, 47.

Then the "show" ended, and the crowd, "the multitudes who assembled to see the sight, when they saw what had taken place, returned home beating their breasts."[31] Who will ever be able to avoid confronting that event? There can be no more indifference. Even Pilate will no longer be able to wash his hands, marveling "that he was already dead." And then, "summoning the centurion, he asked him whether [Jesus] was already dead ... he granted the body to Joseph."[32]

So Jesus really died. The certainty of the centurion's response to Pilate was not the result of opinion or impression, but of verification, when "one of the soldiers pierced [Jesus'] side with a spear, and at once there came out blood and water":[33] the final oblation of His humanity to the Father. Benedict XVI commented that "Jesus' death ... is (however) differentiated from the kind of death resulting from man's original sin as a consequence of his presumption in seeking to be like God," explaining that it "is

---

[31] Luke 23:48.
[32] Mark 15:44–45.
[33] John 19:34.

of another kind: it is occasioned ... by the humility of God.... It is a death in the context of his service of expiation—a death that achieves reconciliation and becomes a light for the nations."[34]

Therefore, in the supreme moment of His existence, Jesus was revealed in His works, in the truth He had proclaimed and in the anguish He suffered. It was His mission. In His real, human, deeply humiliated body, there were no duplicities: "And those who passed by derided him, wagging their heads, and saying, 'Aha! You who would destroy the temple and build it in three days, save yourself, and come down from the cross!... He saved others; he cannot save himself.... Come down now from the cross, that we may see and believe.'"[35] *Who are you? Aren't you a man? Why did you make yourself equal to God?*

In His nakedness, in that tortured body, Christ's full participation[36] in human nakedness was highlighted:

---

[34] Ratzinger, *Jesus of Nazareth*, pp. 252–253.
[35] Mark 15:29–32.
[36] See 2 Cor. 5:21; 1 Pet. 2:22–24; Isa. 53:6.

we are all naked, sinners, before God! He is one of us![37] Still, he is totally other![38]

Since then, we have all needed to be vested in grace, a new nature, while the drama of injustice has never ended.

[37] Among the countless elevated artistic expressions in which Christ crucified has been represented down through the centuries, we would like to mention here one that well expresses the concept of human nakedness in the face of mystery: the *Crucifixion* by the painter Renato Guttuso. The scene shows the Christ hanging on the Cross, naked, as all the protagonists of the scene are naked: the centurion, the two evildoers, the bystanders, and the pious woman who looks at the face of the dead Jesus and, with a delicate gesture, covers His virility, as if to tell everyone that we are the ones who should be ashamed of so much evil! In truth, the artist does not focus on the scandalous and exhibitionist nudity, but on the existentially true nakedness of who we are. If you want another artistic reference, we recommend looking at Marc Chagall's *The White Crucifixion*, painted in 1938; the painter denounces the injustices suffered by the Jewish people, but focuses on the crucified Christ taken as a symbol of the innocent condemned in an unjust manner.

[38] The concept of "totally other" was developed by E. Lévinas, *Totalità e infinito. Saggio sull'esteriorità, Altrimenti che essere* (Milan: Jaca Book 2016).

The Empty Tomb

Together with the Cross, another powerful symbol and shrine that draws devotion in Jerusalem is the place of Jesus' burial.[39] The sepulchre represents that site where the body of the Lord found a home, where the power of God transformed a place of putrefaction into a source of life and grace. The tomb had been ceded by Joseph of Arimathea, who "also was a disciple of Jesus."[40] He had presented himself to Pilate, driven by the need to prevent that venerated and tortured body from being thrown into the mass grave of the executed and to provide a prompt and decent burial before the evening, because the legal rest of the Jewish Passover was about to begin and there was no time to transport it elsewhere. Joseph, with the help of some others, therefore immediately completed the mortuary accommodation of the Master's body, awaiting a better arrangement. After a brief unction with

---

[39] This is a direct reference to the Order, which derives from it not only its title but also its very reason for being.

[40] Matt. 27:57.

the ointments brought by Nicodemus, the body was wrapped in a clean sheet and cloth.[41]

Benedict XVI writes that in the drama that He experienced, Christ "traveled the path of death right to the bitter and seemingly hopeless end in the tomb."[42]

The events recounted by the evangelists stop when the stone is rolled in front of the sepulchral entrance. However, distrust of the words spoken by the Lord during His life had prompted the leaders of the Sanhedrin to place soldiers in front of the entrance with Pilate's consent.[43] Indeed, Jesus had said that He would suffer, be killed, and then rise again.[44] This could have fueled the dim hope of the Resurrection, and that greatly disturbed the peace of the Sanhedrin.

---

[41] According to the evangelist John, Nicodemus brought about a hundred pounds of a mixture of myrrh and aloe (John 19:39), and the evangelist Matthew notes that Joseph wrapped the body in a "clean sheet" (see Matt. 27:59).

[42] Ratzinger, *Jesus of Nazareth*, p. 253.

[43] See Matt. 27:62–66.

[44] See Matt. 16:21.

With the closure of the tomb completed and the entrance blocked with the large stone, the passage was sealed[45] while "Mary Magdalene and the other Mary were there, sitting opposite the sepulchre."[46] In addition to keeping watch over those busy with sealing the tomb, they were unable to detach themselves from their beloved Master. It is precisely because of what they observed that, three days later, when going to the tomb, they asked, "Who will roll away the stone?"[47]

In the sepulchre was the silence of many questions and of the many expectations of those who wanted an explanation of the many whys. There God awaits us, and we learn faith. There was the silence of the "Son of man,"[48] who, having assumed human nature and its transience, had inherited its death. It was not the silence of God.

---

[45] See Matt. 27:66.

[46] Matt. 27:61.

[47] Mark 16:3.

[48] An expression that appears eighty-one times in the four Gospels, always referring to Jesus.

The Resurrection

For three days, silence fell over Jerusalem.

"Now after the sabbath, toward the dawn of the first day of the week,"[49] in front of the empty tomb, again we encounter Mary Magdalene, the first to realize that the entrance had been opened and the body of Jesus was absent. Mary the mother of James, Salome, and Joanna realized the same, and, on having been alerted, Simon Peter and John also came running. The Sanhedrin guards, shaken by a noise like an earthquake, had fled; a corrupt attempt was made to promote the claim that the body had been stolen. This was an absurdity, because the guards had been placed there to prevent exactly this and were not charged.[50]

A voice was heard, a question from which we ourselves cannot flee: "Whom do you seek?"[51]

Mary Magdalene was stunned: the body of Jesus was gone. She wondered: How is this possible? The

---

[49] Matt. 28:1; see also Mark 16:1; Luke 24:1.
[50] See Matt. 27:64; 28:12–14.
[51] John 20:15.

most obvious conclusion was that someone had taken Him away in the night!

The voice asks her: "Whom do you seek?" Jesus calls her by name: Mary! Pure emotion. It is the Master!

According to Luke's account, suddenly "two men ... in dazzling apparel" stood by the frightened women [who had come to the tomb] and said to them, "Why do you seek the living among the dead? He is not here, but has risen."[52]

Another variant of the same question. Whom are you looking for? Whom are you seeking?

Whom are *we* looking for? To Dames and Knights of the Holy Sepulchre: What are you looking for in the Order of the Holy Sepulchre? I think this question arises at least once. It is therefore worthwhile to place yourself mentally in front of the empty tomb and gain firsthand the same experience as Mary Magdalene—perhaps on a pilgrimage, which we are invited to make to the Holy Land at least once in our lives: Why am I here? What did I come to do? Whom am I looking for?

[52] Luke 24:4–6.

No one witnessed the moment of Christ's Resurrection.[53]

The stone had been rolled away.[54] The only ones present, the guards, were so afraid that they "trembled and became like dead men."[55] Someone dressed in white, an angel, said to the women: "Do not be afraid; for I know that you seek Jesus who was crucified. He is not here; for he has risen, as he said. Come, see the place where he lay. Then go quickly and tell his disciples that he has risen from the dead, and behold, he is going before you to Galilee; there you will see him. Lo, I have told you."[56]

The Risen One would meet them that day;[57] it was necessary to appease the souls in turmoil, to overcome their amazement and fright.[58] It is true that Mary Magdalene recounted[59] how she had recognized him

---

[53] See Ricciotti, *Vita di Gesù Cristo*, p. 701.

[54] See Matt. 28:2.

[55] Matt. 28:4.

[56] Matt. 28:5–7; see also Mark 16:5–7; Luke 24:5–10.

[57] See Matt. 28:9.

[58] See Matt. 28:4; John 20:1ff.

[59] See Mark 16:9–10; John 20:11–18. Mary Magdalene also tells how she had tried to touch the feet of the Risen One and how He had withdrawn. In fact, Jesus

alive—"Rabboni" (Teacher)[60]—and that the other women spoke of an apparition of angels; but a real encounter with the living Jesus was necessary for His disciples, considering, moreover, that Peter and John had seen in the tomb the sheets and the shroud, His "linen cloths lying ... the napkin, which had been on his head ... rolled up in a place by itself."[61] The argument of the theft of the corpse was not a solid one: Why would thieves steal a dead man without the clothes in which he was wrapped? And was the hypothesis of a risen Jesus credible? And why would He leave [the tomb] naked?

Jesus, therefore, appeared to the women and the disciples and "presented himself alive after his passion by many proofs, appearing to them during forty days, and speaking of the kingdom of God."[62]

---

had not returned to His previous biological life, in which He would still have had to die, but neither was He a ghost; it is an event that shatters the forms of life that we know, and, Ratzinger explains, "matter itself is remolded into a new type of reality." Ratzinger, *Jesus of Nazareth*, p. 274.

[60] John 20:16.

[61] John 20:7.

[62] Acts 1:3.

The Resurrection of Christ in the Christian faith represents the most ontologically extraordinary event; it belongs to the "DNA" of that faith and is the paradigmatic reversal of our arduous human destiny, with its salvific crowning. It is the beginning of preaching and is at the root of the institution of the Church itself, because if Christ had not risen, according to St. Paul, our faith would be in vain.[63] Benedict XVI commented that "the resurrection is the crucial point" of the whole question of faith; adding: "whether Jesus merely was or whether he also is—this depends on the Resurrection"[64]; if Christ had not risen,

> if in Jesus' Resurrection we were dealing simply with the miracle of a resuscitated corpse, it would ultimately be of no concern to us. For it

[63] See 1 Cor. 15:17. All of chapter 15 of this Pauline letter is a broad and accurate catechesis on the death and Resurrection of Jesus, His message of salvation, and the doctrine on the believer's participation in the mystery of the resurrection; as redeemed, the believer "with his body enters the glory of the resurrection, even if the form of existence will be completely different from the current." *La Sacra Bibbia*, CEI-UELCI, p. 1814. Translated from the Italian.

[64] Ratzinger, *Jesus of Nazareth*, p. 242.

would be no more important than the resuscitation of a clinically dead person through the art of doctors. For the world as such and for our human existence, nothing would have changed. The miracle of a resuscitated corpse would indicate that Jesus' Resurrection was equivalent to the raising of the son of the widow of Nain ..., the daughter of Jairus ..., and Lazarus.[65]

For Pope Benedict, the Resurrection of the Son of Man is "utterly different" from other forms of life or revitalization. It was "an entirely new form of life, into a life that is no longer subject to the law of dying and becoming ... a life that opens up a new dimension of human existence ... a universal event."[66] Jesus Himself, therefore, "links faith in the resurrection to his own person: 'I am the resurrection and the life' (John 11:25)."[67]

Consequently, the empty sepulchre, on further reflection, is not and does not represent for the Christian a simple burial place, like so many others. This

[65] Ratzinger, *Jesus of Nazareth*, p. 243.
[66] Ratzinger, *Jesus of Nazareth*, p. 244.
[67] *Catechism of the Catholic Church* (CCC), no. 994.

would perhaps have affected archaeology, but not the Christian faith, nor would an institution like the Church have arisen. It is not even a symbol. Rather, it is evidence of a drama that had taken place against a man condemned by the obstinacy of a religious power and by the ineptitude of those who represented the power of Rome in Palestine at the time. Due to the Resurrection of Jesus, it is the conclusion of a life, which began in a manger[68] and ended with burial.

Beyond the tomb, there is the beginning of a new adventure, of another totally different life, which opens to a sense of faith: one can believe, or one cannot believe; this is the human dilemma. Yet faith does not flourish without the intervention and help of grace, which must be asked for.[69] Indeed, among the first who "believed" in the Resurrection of Jesus we also find the guards, scared and fleeing, and those in the Sanhedrin, who had to pay the guards to claim it was a theft![70] All of them, however, remained closed in a sad and heavy blindness. Christian faith, the first of

[68] See Luke 2:12.
[69] "Apart from me you can do nothing" (John 15:5).
[70] Saint Augustine, not without irony, would have asked: How come you bring sleeping witnesses?

the theological virtues, arises from the mystery of the Lord's Resurrection. It is linked to it and presupposes humility of intelligence; the life that welcomes the Risen One will lead every believer to "be a witness to Christ ... a 'witness of his resurrection' (Acts 1:22)."[71]

In relation to this rich theology of the *mysterium crucis* and the *mysterium gloriosum resurrectionis*, since the beginning of the life of the Church, the desire to make pilgrimages to and to live near the places of the Lord's memory has historically asserted itself in a growing way: if I cannot meet the Lord *de visu*, if my desire to see Him cannot be satisfied — like those Greeks who requested of the apostle Philip, "We wish to see Jesus"[72] — is it not at least possible to see the places where He lived, died, and rose again?[73]

---

[71] CCC 995.

[72] John 12:21.

[73] History is full of pilgrims who have visited or stopped in Palestine and have left us memoirs of great value for the understanding and perception of the Faith over the centuries. Men and women, such as the pilgrim from Bordeaux (333); St. Jerome, who went to live in the Holy Land (386); Egeria, who left us a *Peregrinatio ad loca Sancta* (383); St. Helen, who went to search for the Cross of the Lord, and her son Constantine,

Peace Be with You! A Message for Always

To greet someone is a gesture of great courtesy. Jesus does not attempt to evade it. Yet a formal greeting in itself is not enough; rather, the content, the tone of voice, the meeting and holding of the gaze, the grasping of a serene facial expression or the lack thereof: these are the essential signs to help us understand who stands in front of us and, above all, what he holds in his heart. Jesus greets the disciples, who were intimidated, locked in the house for fear of the Jews, scattered by events and their own behavior. They doubt whether the friendship of the Lord, declared

---

who erected a basilica above the sepulchre (fourth century); Empress Eudoxia, who settled in Jerusalem (fifth century); St. Francis of Assisi, attracted by the Lord and wanting to follow in His footsteps (1219); St. Bridget of Sweden, the mystic of the Passion of the Lord (1372); and so, like a river in flood, many faithful to the present day; I limit myself here to remembering the pilgrimage of Paul VI (1964), the first pope to visit the Holy Land, with the historic embrace of forgiveness between him and the Patriarch Athenagoras; of John Paul II (2000); of Benedict XVI (2009); and of Francis (2014). The line of pilgrims of all ages and times is without end.

on another occasion,[74] is still intact. At the greeting, "Peace be with you!" they "were glad"![75]

In fact, the voice of the Risen One was reassuring, the hands with the sign of the nails and the pierced side were His own: Jesus was alive! And this was the most important thing for them: He was truly alive and was not a ghost! Even Thomas wanted to have the same incredible experience of the Risen One. And to us, deprived of the same possibility, Jesus bequeathed a beatitude that they, the disciples, could not enjoy: "Blessed are those who have not seen and yet believe."[76]

But now Jesus needs to recover His friends so He may entrust them with continuing His mission. He gathers them all to Him again, everyone, men and women, including those who, leaving Jerusalem, were going to Emmaus, disappointed and sad.[77] However, He will ask the Eleven to be His witnesses, apostles, in the world.

[74] See John 15:15.
[75] John 20:19–20.
[76] John 20:29.
[77] See Luke 24:13–35.

We cannot forget that, when Jesus wished peace upon them, that greeting did not concern only those to whom it was addressed, since the word *peace* is part of the name of Jerusalem (City of Peace),[78] a city that was intensely loved by the Lord and that He had known from childhood. He especially loved His Temple, the heart of the city. He had even intervened vigorously on its behalf, driving out those who had made it a market.[79] And in the last days of His life, Jesus had cried over Jerusalem, "Would that even today you knew the things that make for peace!"[80]

As Members of the Order of the Holy Sepulchre, we are not insensitive to the Lord's sentiments, and we are aware of a special love for this city, in the not secondary dream of promoting the inclusiveness of the rights of all those who live there and of the pilgrims;

[78] See Gen. 14:18. Melchizedek is said to be the king of Salem (Peace) who offers bread and wine on the return of Abraham from the war; the author of the Letter to the Hebrews saw Jesus, "Son of God ... a priest forever" (Heb. 7:1–3), and Psalm 76:2 proclaimed: Salem the "tent of God" and Zion His "dwelling place."

[79] See Matt. 21:12–13; Mark 11:15–19; Luke 19:45–48; John 2:13–17.

[80] Luke 19:42.

respect for rights, in fact, represents the pavement for the path of peace in the Holy Land. We are committed, so to speak, to "shedding" a tear for the Land and the "city of the great King."[81] We will not be the great architects of peace and civil coexistence; rather, resorting to a well-known evangelical image, we prefer to be small workers in the Lord's vineyard[82] — not presumptuous, not all-knowing, but happy craftsmen, believing that, in this way, we can make a real and effective contribution, even if [it is] not always visible or recognized by most. If it is up to everyone to contribute to peace, for us the commitment is primary, and we make it a serious reason for our belonging to the Order. It is a great honor!

Jerusalem and the Holy Land are, for many, the places of an ideal historical reference; the presence

---

[81] Matt. 5:35; in Psalm 48:2, Mount Zion (Jerusalem) is sung as "a wonderful hill ... joy of all the earth," "a divine dwelling," "city of the great Sovereign." Isaiah also proclaimed joy for Jerusalem, the holy city, which he exhorted to put on splendid clothes for the coming of the "messenger who announces peace" (see Isa. 52:1–7).

[82] See Matt. 20:1ff.

of numerous Christian and non-Christian confessions manifests the good that the international community desires for them. Finally, we cannot forget that Jerusalem is the figure of another Jerusalem, the heavenly one, messianically glimpsed in the Old Testament by the prophets Isaiah (who indicated her as "Bride of the Lord"[83]) and Baruch (who had urged her to lay down her garments of mourning and affliction and vest in the splendor of glory that comes from God forever);[84] in the New Testament Saint Paul calls her "our mother."[85]

Emmaus: from the Side of the Disciples

"That very day two of them were going to a village named Emmaus, about seven miles from Jerusalem,

[83] See Isa. 54:1–17.

[84] See Bar. 5:1–9.

[85] Gal. 4:26. Even the author of the Letter to the Hebrews does not exempt himself from speaking of the "heavenly Jerusalem," in which the "firstborn whose names are written in the heavens" gather joyfully (see Heb. 12:22–23), and the book of Revelation exalts her as "Bride of the Lamb," a glorious figure of the Church (see Rev. 21:9–27).

and talking with each other about all these things that had happened. While they were talking and discussing together, Jesus himself drew near and went with them. But their eyes were kept from recognizing him."[86]

This passage from Luke's Gospel represents the prototype of every experience of faith before Christ: His humanity, the expectations about His words and promises, the meaning of His violent death, the Resurrection and, finally, His divinity. It is a paradigmatic step of all spirituality. Nonetheless, it applies to every Dame and Knight who, in the journey of faith in Jesus, sometimes suffers moments of crisis and spiritual winter.

The Emmaus passage, therefore, is a distinctly cat-echetical one, seen "from the side" of the disciples and of every man and woman who intends to follow Christ. Thus, in this sense, it is an icon of our lives: the two disciples are we, and the road to the village (Emmaus) is our lives. The conversations represent our dialogue about the meaning of events, about our existence, and about our knowledge of and relation-ship with God. Their hopes are ours, their perplexities

[86] Luke 24:13–16.

and human and spiritual expectations are ours, and the drama (the death of Christ) and the unpredictable (the Resurrection) are part of our experience.

In this existential dynamic, what is the key to everything? Is there one? This is the search that will accompany us always and everywhere and from which no one can escape. If there is no key, if there is no answer, the crisis will be perennial.

On the road to Emmaus — that is, toward the meaning of our existence — Jesus offers the key to open eyes and mind, reprimanding the two disciples: "How slow of heart to believe!"[87] His death, he explains, occurred in the sign of redemption. It does not belong to the line of Adam's sin. It is "a death that achieves reconciliation and becomes a light for the nations,"[88] explains Benedict XVI. In our lives, God is not an indifferent spectator; Jesus does not remain buried by death and our unbelief. He is alive and accompanies us travelers. He makes Himself known in the signs of the spirit; He "warms" the heart, giving meaning to our questions; He "sits" at the table

[87] See Luke 24:25.
[88] Ratzinger, *Jesus of Nazareth*, p. 253.

with us; He "takes" and "breaks" the bread of faith; He "pronounces" the blessing; He "gives us" the food of the sacraments, of forgiveness, and grace; and He allows our eyes slowly to "open." But we will not be able to recognize Him except in the humility and obedience of faith itself, in the footsteps of the poor, in the footprints of the marginalized and the victims of abuse and violence. Then He "pushes" us to return to Jerusalem, the city of life (sacred and profane) par excellence, to testify that we have encountered Jesus and that the empty sepulchre is the void of our human expectations, of the idolatry of things, of the selfishness that suffocates, the contamination of hatred, empty pride.

It can be said that, like the disciples [on the road to] Emmaus, the recognition of Jesus is a recognition that starts from within, as the two disciples affirm: they "said to each other, 'Did not our hearts burn within us while he talked to us on the road, while he opened to us the scriptures?' "[89] Recognizing Jesus as the Lord, the Christ who saves, is certainly the result of events and people around us, but all this does not exhaust our

[89] Luke 24:32.

understanding of it, if we do not recognize the role of grace that precedes and accompanies us. Faith always remains, deep down, shrouded in mystery where the initiative of God and human initiative intersect, a constant in every experience from Abraham onward.

In the Boat with Peter

John places this story after Christ's Resurrection, when He had sent His disciples back to Galilee where He would encounter them again. Galilee is the place where it all began, and for the disciples, it would have been the least traumatic region—a return to the freshness of their first call from Jesus.

Peter and [a few] other disciples went fishing at night, but they had caught nothing. At dawn, Jesus waited for them on the shore, [although they did not know it was He]. He asked if they had caught any-thing, and, [told that they had not], He invited them to throw their net on the other side of the boat; and their catch was so incredibly abundant that they were left in no doubt that the person was the Master.

There, before the sea of Galilee, Jesus obtained from Peter his triple attestation of love: "Lord, you know everything; you know that I love you,"[90] he confessed with intense and intimate emotion; and Jesus entrusted him with the responsibility of the Church. That was the moment when, one might think, the Master glimpsed the long line of Peter's successors who would continue his mission.

There will never be an expression of love simpler and more beautiful than that of Peter, because it presupposes the sincerity of heart of the one who pronounces it, the recognition of one's weakness and the appeal to Christ, who knows the depths of each person. Mine and yours too. Peter, matured from a past of impulses and betrayal, will not forget that he will always have to trust in Christ. Saint Augustine, one of the greatest Fathers of the Church, wrote that Peter "as a person ... was only a man; on the level of grace he was certainly a Christian, but on the higher level of grace he was the only and same Prince of the apostles."[91]

[90] John. 21:15–17.
[91] Augustine, *Trattati su Giovanni*, Tratt. 124, 5; *Corpus Christianorum Latinorum* (CCL) (Belgium: Brepols, 1953), 36, p. 685. Translation from the Italian.

Being with Peter, to whom Jesus entrusts His flock — "feed my lambs; feed my sheep"[92] — is for us of the Order of the Holy Sepulchre a principle of identity, to detach us from "the heroism of [our] personal deeds and learn the humility of the disciple"[93] in fidelity to Christ and the Successor of Peter.

Where Peter is, there is the Church, affirmed St. Ambrose. It is upon the profession of faith of Peter — "You are the Christ, the Son of the living God"[94] — that Jesus builds His Church. St. Paul, in fact, clarifies, "For no other foundation can any one lay than that which is laid, which is Jesus Christ,"[95] and Peter has Christ as His foundation. The Church, therefore, received from Christ, "in the person of Peter, the keys of the kingdom of heaven, that is, the power to dissolve and bind sins, and this Church loves and follows Christ, and for this she is freed from evils."[96] Even if sometimes the "boat" of the Church finds

[92] See John 21:15–17.
[93] Ratzinger, *Jesus of Nazareth*, p. 71.
[94] Matt. 16:16.
[95] 1 Cor. 3:11.
[96] Augustine, *Trattati*, p. 685. Translation from the Italian.

itself navigating stormy and agitated waves, so as to give the impression of the waves' having the upper hand, we must never forget that the Lord is always "there, and he comes (and intervenes) at the right moment. 'I go, and come to you'—that is the essence of Christian trust, the reason for our joy,"[97] that is, the joy of bearing witness to Jesus, Who saves to the ends of the world, even at the cost of persecution and sometimes even to death.

At Jacob's Well: Water to Quench Our Thirst

Jesus is in Samaria, in the region between Judea and Galilee. In Sychar is the well-known well that Jacob has left to his son Joseph. It is noon, and there is no one there. Jesus is thirsty, and the disciples have gone to the village to buy food. A woman comes to draw water, and Jesus asks her for a drink; in fact, she has a bucket for drawing water. A dialogue takes place between Jesus and the woman, one that is far from trivial. The woman is amazed that a Jew should speak with a Samaritan woman but also that Jesus speaks

[97] Ratzinger, *Jesus of Nazareth*, p. 285.

strangely of a water that she does not have, though the well is deep and He does not have a container to draw from it. Jesus explains to her that He speaks of another water that gushes forth for eternal life and that, to have it, one must pursue the truth in life: the man with whom she lives is not her husband! Then he speaks to her of the salvation that comes from God and [explains] that God must be worshipped in spirit and truth.[98]

The well recalls the story of Joseph, lowered into a waterless cistern by envious brothers to be abandoned to death. He is providentially saved by merchants, who buy him and bring him to Egypt. Joseph's well and his sad story recall by analogy that of Jesus, condemned out of envy and betrayed by one of His own for money; that well is a symbol of the sepulchre of Jesus, which, after He was taken down from the Cross, briefly guarded the life that had been taken away. A new life was about to "gush" forth again, however. Since time immemorial, water is life.[99]

[98] See John 4:1–30.
[99] Not only in an analogical sense; in the Middle East, atrocious wars were fought to control water resources,

The sepulchre in which Jesus was placed after His death, and in whose "depths" the great mystery of new life was rising, was ready to explode and truly to allow a new existence to emerge that "surpasses knowledge," teaches St. Paul.[100] Moses, bewildered because the people in the desert murmured against God and against him for the lack of water and doubted that water could simply flow from a rock, hit it twice with his stick,[101] and water gushed. That wounded rock became an image of Christ's pierced side, from which "a spring of water welling up to eternal life" would flow.[102]

A Dame and a Knight, through their commitment to the Order, know that, with their promise, they ideally approach that well. From that deep source, that is, from that "sepulchre," the new life, the Risen Christ, gushed forth. From Him comes all truth and spiritual

---

and hatreds that have never since healed have been fomented.

[100] Eph. 3:19.

[101] See Num. 20:6–13. Moses did not believe that, by the word of God, water could flow for the people; therefore, he struck [the rock] twice with his stick.

[102] John 4:14.

knowledge. The empty tomb therefore speaks to us of the living Master, Whom the apostle Thomas recognizes and confesses — "My Lord and my God"[103] — and Whom the Church is always called to testify to and to announce to all peoples and at all times. A Dame and a Knight also know that they must continually draw spiritual energy and enthusiasm from the empty tomb of Christ whenever they need it, because it is from that "well," from that open "rock," from that "spring," that love for one's faith and commitment to the Land of Jesus flows. Faith is a gift and a task: a gift, as we are gratuitously saved by Christ; a task, in that it makes us active in witnessing to Him, present in the poor and in the corporal works of mercy.

[103] John 20:28.

The Ecclesiological Dimension
of Spirituality

Baptismal Grace

Water is also a reminder of Baptism and brings us back to the Risen Lord, to Easter in the sense of the passage from death to supernatural life and grace. It sacramentally confers on us the dignity of children of God. We must never forget that the dignity granted to us by the Church therefore comes from Baptism, which is at its very root.

In life, however, we are not immune from the risk of losing or rejecting the mystery of the Risen Lord's grace. It is enough to observe the reactions in front of the empty tomb (the empty tomb for a Member of the Order is always a school of wisdom). Not everyone behaved the same way or drew the same conclusions: the guards, positioned to prevent the corpse of Christ from being stolen, fled frightened and allowed themselves to be bribed to affirm a falsehood. The heads and religious leaders of the Jerusalem Temple continued to plot by denying the evidence of the Risen One provided by the guards. The disciples were wrought by a psychological fragility, caught between doubt and disbelief over the events that had overwhelmed them; yet, "when they saw him [the Risen Lord] they worshiped him."[1] Finally, Mary Magdalene and the women who accompanied her were initially surprised, but then, "they departed quickly from the tomb with fear and great joy, and ran to tell his disciples."[2]

Among whom would we wish to be counted? When faith is shaken, among whom would we like to be? If we took for granted that these questions do not concern us, as baptized [Catholics], we would miss an extraordinary opportunity to give a profound meaning to our faith: that is, to experience the Risen Lord personally. We need to stay there, in front of the

[1] Matt. 28:17.
[2] Matt. 28:8.

sepulchre that welcomed like a womb the body of Jesus, ready to be generated a second time, with the same humility, the same affection, and the same inner desire of Mary Magdalene and the other women.

Perceiving in my spirit that Jesus calls me by name; that, for Him, I am not an anonymous person; that God is the living God, as the prophet Elijah perceived him on Horeb in the whisper of "a gentle breeze,"[3] is a unique experience that marks me for a lifetime. God exists and I encountered him, was the affirmation of a former atheist philosopher.[4]

From that moment on, the time for witness comes. Mary Magdalene would have liked to restrain Jesus, to touch Him physically; but He was no longer as in the past: "the earlier way of relating to the earthly Jesus is no longer possible,"[5] because, according to Paul, "from now on, therefore, we regard no one from a human point of view; even though we once regarded Christ

[3] See 1 Kings 19:12.

[4] It is also the title of the story of his conversion by A. Frossard (1969), who says that he, an atheist, encountered God one day in the silence of a church he had entered by chance.

[5] Ratzinger, *Jesus of Nazareth*, p. 285.

from a human point of view, we regard him thus no longer."[6] What remains, then, is to open our minds to the Scriptures,[7] to believe and proclaim it like Mary Magdalene, who went to say to the disciples: "I have seen the Lord!"[8] It would then be up to them to witness to the Risen One and bring Baptism to the ends of the earth: "Go therefore and make disciples of all nations, baptizing them in the name of the Father and of the Son and of the Holy Spirit."[9]

In life, we will often be tormented by our doubts and rebellions, because, as St. Paul says, we are faced with the "secret and hidden wisdom of God, which God decreed before the ages for our glorification"[10] — that is, Christ, Whose mission and word do not belong to so-called human reasonableness; just as we will be humiliated by our sins and the evils that afflict us. Bewildered, we lose the sense of God's pedagogy toward us, although He educates us continually and never ceases to love us.

[6] 2 Cor. 5:16.
[7] See Luke 24:44-45.
[8] John 20:18.
[9] Matt. 28:19.
[10] 1 Cor. 2:7.

It would be fascinating for us to think of belonging to the group of Mary and the other women comforted by the Risen One, where true fidelity to God is found in righteousness of heart, in whose depth we will always be plumbed as Dames and Knights of the Holy Sepulchre. In the company of Peter, whom Jesus asks three times if he loved Him, and replying like him, mindful of his fragility, "Lord, you know everything; you know that I love you,"[11] is where we would like to be — and to have the certainty that on Peter Jesus wanted to build His Church firmly, accompanied by the Holy Spirit.

Jesus, the Word of God

In the Christian life, we can never forget that the Word of God remains forever and that this Word "entered into time. God spoke his eternal Word humanly; his Word 'became flesh' (*Jn* 1:14). This is the good news. This is the proclamation which has come down

[11] John 21:17.

the centuries to us today."[12] The Gospels—which "faithfully hand on what Jesus Christ, while living among men, really did and taught for their eternal salvation"[13]—reveal first of all the mystery of the Person together with His teaching, which, without a shadow of a doubt, is theologically and anthropologically the highest known in human wisdom.

St. Paul, citing the prophet Isaiah—"I will destroy the wisdom of the wise; the intelligence of the intelligent I will frustrate"—reiterates that God has a plan for humanity, a plan that the world, with all its wisdom, has not known and that affirms that "the word of the cross ... the power of God" is what saved us.[14] This is why we always approach the Word of God, as the Fathers of the Second Vatican Council write in the constitution *Dei Verbum*, with a sense of "reverence,"[15] since it is precisely the Person of Jesus.

---

[12] Benedict XVI, Post-Synodal Apostolic Exhortation *Verbum Domini* (VD) (September 30, 2010), no. 1.

[13] Second Vatican Council, Dogmatic Constitution on Divine Revelation *Dei Verbum* (DV) (November 18, 1965), no. 19.

[14] 1 Cor. 1:15–21.

[15] *DV*, no. 1.

He allows us to know, or better introduces us to, the knowledge of the Father and gives us the Holy Spirit, the Source of all good. At the same time, it allows us to enjoy the unitary and Trinitarian life of God. We know that the Church itself is, moreover, founded and inhabited by Trinitarian love and that the grace of Baptism is given to us in the same Trinitarian dimension: "Go therefore and make disciples of all nations, baptizing them in the name of the Father and of the Son and of the Holy Spirit."[16] Christian life and the sacraments are therefore an expression of the Trinitarian life, and all preaching can only be Trinitarian.

In the Apostolic Exhortation *Verbum Domini*, following the 2008 synod of bishops, Benedict XVI wrote that "the novelty of biblical revelation consists in the fact that God becomes known through the dialogue which he desires to have with us."[17] This is why the Logos, the Word of God, entered the world and assumed human nature, so that the dialogue could take place in an understandable and direct form. Here we are reminded of the expressions of the Letter to the

[16] Matt. 28:19–20.
[17] *VD*, no. 6.

Hebrews, whose author teaches that God has always spoken in many ways and forms, including through the prophets, but that "in these last days he has spoken to us by a Son."[18] Jesus of Nazareth is the Word Who has made Himself audible and has taken on a face through Mary. The Paschal Mystery is, then, the salvific fulfillment that St. Paul identifies in the Cross. The Church, therefore, is born from the Word of Christ, lives by the announcement of the same Word, and proclaims it by projecting itself into the world at the service of the Word itself.

In the Order of the Holy Sepulchre, listening to the Word of God, as a Trinitarian gift of salvation, remains fundamental in the context of a biblically founded spirituality; without this, one would remain dry and formalistic.

Commitment: Prayer and Eucharist

Prayer should never be missing from our lives. In the family of Nazareth, Jesus learned to pray and practiced [prayer] in the Jewish style in the synagogue of His

[18] Heb. 1:2.

village. Prayer belongs to the life of Jesus, and this aroused in the disciples the desire to imitate Him. And so, He not only recommended it but also taught how to pray.[19] The Our Father, the prayer par excellence, became its content and guide. The Lord then also taught how to pray: without hypocrisy, in confidentiality, without wasting words. Lastly, "keeping vigil" in prayer appears in the Gospels as an evident constant of the Lord before the most important moments.[20] Thus, the night before His Passion, the Lord asked His disciples to keep vigil and pray together with Him.[21]

Praying per se also belongs to the style and nature of our Order. Therefore, every Dame or Knight is well advised to learn to pray and to do so constantly. In fact, faith is expressed in prayer—not *our* faith, but that of Jesus, to which we are attached. Always in prayer we must also ask Him to allow us to unite with Him to address the Father together and obtain the gift of the Holy Spirit, according to the splendid teaching of St. Augustine, who said that the Lord Jesus "prays

[19] See Luke 11:1–4; Matt. 6:5–13.
[20] See Luke 6:12; Matt. 14:23; Mark 1:35.
[21] See Matt. 26:36, 40.

for us, as our Priest; He prays in us, as our Head; He is prayed to by us, as our God."[22]

But there is yet another commitment that must be dear to the Members of the Order: the Eucharist. It is the most precious gift left by Jesus to His disciples, whom He asked to repeat it: "Do this in remembrance of me."[23] In the Sacrament of the Eucharist, *Mysterium fidei*, He placed Himself at the center, at the heart of the Church. We are understandably speaking of the "ecclesial prayer" par excellence, which develops, more than any other, the sense of fraternal communion: the Eucharist, the mystery of the Body and Blood of the Lord Jesus, in which the sacrifice of the Cross is sacramentally perpetuated. The Eucharist was entrusted to His Church as a memorial of His death and Resurrection, and this happened in the most emotional moment of the relationship between Jesus and the disciples, when He was about to take leave of them. Then something new happened and will happen forever, in every place and time in

[22] See St. Augustine, Exposition on Psalm 86, CCL 39, 1176–1177.
[23] Luke 22:19; 1 Cor. 11:24–25.

which the same gesture of "breaking the bread" will be repeated. A New Covenant was extended to all humanity. The Eucharist, therefore, in the Church is "the source and summit of the Christian life"[24]. A Dame and a Knight should never neglect to participate in the Eucharist. There is no more perfect and elevated act of worship than this, and it is always an act of blessing and thanksgiving.

We also like to think that in the adoration of the Eucharist, the gesture of Mary of Bethany, who, in humility and great affection, anointed the feet of the Lord, is prolonged, so to speak. This gesture was appreciated by the Lord in view of His death, just as a similar gesture, that of the woman forgiven in the house of Simon the Pharisee, had been appreciated.[25] As gestures of love, they can no longer dissipate, and indeed, they continue to perpetuate themselves in eucharistic adoration, together with charity toward the poor, children, refugees, prisoners, marginalized people, suffering people: "Truly, I say to you, as you did it to one of the least of these my brethren, you did

---

[24] CCC 1324; see CCC 1322–1327.
[25] See Luke 7:36–50.

it to me."[26] The Eucharist and charity have become inseparable.

The Mystery of Charity

"The principal driving force behind the authentic development of every person and of all humanity," wrote Benedict XVI in one of the most beautiful documents of his pontificate, is charity "to which Jesus Christ bore witness by his earthly life and especially by his death and resurrection.... [It] is an extraordinary force which leads people to opt for courageous and generous engagement in the field of justice and peace."[27] It is a question here of understanding that the root of charity is Christ: His life, His teaching, the signs that accompanied Him, His Passion, death, and Resurrection. In fact, according to the apostle Peter, Jesus "went about doing good and healing all that were oppressed by the devil."[28] The parables of

[26] Matt. 25:40.
[27] Benedict XVI, Encyclical Letter *Caritas in Veritate* (June 29, 2009), no. 1; see also Benedict XVI, Encyclical Letter *Deus Caritas Est* (December 25, 2005).
[28] Acts 10:38.

Christ about humanity, mercy, love for the least, in truth do not formalize a theory but express the meaning of charity itself in a masterly way, as love received and given.[29] In this giving and receiving, Paul VI also taught, the true development of man takes place because solidarity "brings us ... benefits" and, at the same time, "obligations"[30] — above all, against the selfish claim that we owe nothing to anyone except ourselves and that we have only rights. Charity is better understood when we ourselves experience the need: first of all, spiritual (when we lose the sense of God and seem to experience a lack of sense to life), but also moral (so evident in the humiliation due to our sins) or psychological (when depression makes us prisoners, unable to react, and [our] darkened mind makes our strength fail); and no less in situations of economic poverty (when we are reduced to misery).

Thus, Jesus never speaks in defense of charity. He shows it concretely in reference to people in need: the poor, the sick, the woman accused of adultery, the

[29] See Benedict XVI, *Caritas in Veritate*, no. 5.

[30] Paul VI, Encyclical Letter *Populorum Progressio* (March 26, 1967), no. 17.

possessed; and also the expert in the law who asked him: "Who is my neighbor?"[31] Jesus gives him no explanations but tells the parable of the good Samaritan, about a man who, going down from Jerusalem to Jericho, was set upon by brigands who robbed him, beat him, and abandoned him half-dead; only a Samaritan took care of him. The conclusion was obvious: "Go and do likewise."[32]

Christ's gesture on the Cross is that of the highest charity. When He welcomes the repentance of the thief crucified next to him and then asks the Father not to impute His own death to His killers, we are faced with "sacramental" charity, which the priest exercises in the highest degree in the Sacrament of Confession. Like the apostles, Paul will also experience Christ's merciful charity firsthand. For this reason, he will be able to write one of the most beautiful texts on this theological virtue to the Corinthians. It is a text that every Member of the Order of the Holy Sepulchre of Jerusalem should know well:

[31] Luke 10:29.
[32] Luke 10:37.

If I speak in the tongues of men and of angels ... if I have prophetic powers ... and if I have all faith, so as to remove mountains ... if I give away all I have, and if I deliver my body to be burned, but have not love, I gain nothing. Love is patient and kind; love is not jealous or boastful; it is not arrogant or rude. Love does not insist on its own way; it is not irritable or resentful; it does not rejoice at wrong, but rejoices in the right. Love ... endures all things.[33]

Together with the witness of faith, charity also prolongs Christ's presence in the world if love of neighbor is rooted in the love of God. It is a task that concerns each of the faithful, but, at the same time, belongs to the entire ecclesial community, from the local one to the universal Church in Her entirety. As Members of the Order of the Holy Sepulchre, we are involved for two reasons: because we are children of the Church and because we are bound to a noble pastoral-charitable institution that shows specific attention to the needs of the Holy Land. In this way, we carry out, as our bond,

[33] 1 Cor. 13:1–7.

an ordered service to the common good in the Land of Christ: to the Christian families residing there, to the coexistence with the various religious communities in addition to the Catholic one, to the education of children and young people without distinction of creed, and finally, to the pilgrims who intend to travel to the places and relive the most important words and moments in the life of Jesus.

The commitment of the Order to the Patriarchal Church of Jerusalem is now of significant importance and is in line with what is recalled by both the Acts of the Apostles — all the believers had all things in common and shared with each other according to each person's needs[34] — and the apostle Paul, who, in

[34] See Acts 2:44–45. If every Christian has a duty to exercise charity, and this implies that they are called to be the bulwark of the defenseless, suffering, vulnerable people, the Knight and the Dame are called to be so to a greater degree by concretely applying the teaching of Jesus: "'Lord, when did we see thee hungry and feed thee, or thirsty and give thee drink? And when did we see thee a stranger and welcome thee, or naked and clothe thee? And when did we see thee sick or in prison and visit thee?' And the King will answer them, 'Truly, I say to you, as you did it to one of the

moments of particular calamity, of persecution, and of famine, asked the communities of Antioch, Greece, Galatia, and Macedonia to remember the "saints" in Jerusalem and to hold collections, which he later described as generous, indeed "beyond their ability."[35] We therefore perceive, in this common commitment, one of our characteristic "traits," which allows each Member of the Order to exercise his spirituality through "a marked generosity" drawn from [his] "own

---

least of these my brethren, you did it to me.'" (Matt. 25:37–40).

[35] In the Acts of the Apostles it is mentioned that with commendable zeal the first Christians of Antioch, "determined, every one according to his ability, to send relief to the brethren who lived in Judea" because of the serious famine that occurred between 49 and 50, "in the days of Claudius," so they sent their help "by the hand of Barnabas and Saul" (11:27–30). It was a gesture of high solidarity, no less than that of the Churches of Galatia, Corinth (see 1 Cor. 16:1–4), and Macedonia, whose faithful, despite "their extreme poverty," had shown great generosity. The apostle Paul writes in his second Letter to the Corinthians, "For they gave according to their means, as I can testify, and beyond their means, of their own free will, begging us earnestly for the favor of taking part in the relief of the saints" (2 Cor. 8:3–4).

material ... resources."[36] It is worthwhile remembering the words of Pope St. Leo the Great: "May generosity be given to the poor and the suffering so that thanks may be given to God. And may it happen with joy."[37] The joy of doing good!

Therefore, membership in the Order[38] does not imply membership in "a philanthropic entity committed to promoting the material and social improvement of

[36] See in this regard article 4 of the Constitution, which lists the following "Commitments": personal renunciation, generosity, courage, solidarity, concern, involvement of the Members of the Order, and cooperation.
[37] St. Leo the Great, *Discorsi* (no. 10) *sulla Quaeresima*, 3-5, *PL* 54, pp. 299–301. Translated from the Italian.
[38] It should be noted that today our institution is not always well understood; sometimes, on the contrary, it is judged unnecessary or not in keeping with modern reality, almost as if it is a reserve for a caste of vain and anachronistic people. In the often predominant banality or uniformity of the current mentality, reference is not made to a "vocation" with high ethical, spiritual, and humanitarian purposes, nor is the contribution given to safeguarding the coexistence of Christian and non-Christian communities in the sacred places properly grasped, or the protection of a historical-cultural tradition that belongs to everyone, properly grasped.

recipients."[39] Rather, it means having the conviction of the spiritual value of one's membership and, at the same time, of the very high value of charity. This twofold perception should never fail. Being a Knight or Dame[40] of the Order of the Holy Sepulchre, in fact, implies developing the double profile just mentioned, rooted in faith in Christ, Who died and rose again, without making membership depend on occasional events, personal aspects, or crises, present in every organization.

An Ecclesial Reality

Belonging to the Order of the Holy Sepulchre of Jerusalem does not take place outside the Church, but within it.[41] The solemn liturgy of Investiture is like its

---

[39] Francis, *Address to Members of the Consulta.*

[40] The terminology recalls analogies with the past and in some way welcomes its virtues and moral values, which characterized the chivalric orders of the past; today, however, Members are called to place "evangelical love of neighbour as the central and final aim of your works, to bear witness everywhere to the goodness and care with which God loves everyone." Ibid.

[41] The first pastoral reference for each Member of the Order is his or her parish and diocese. Although, by

apex. This event is not a simple honorific attribution. The Order — as is known — has a mission entrusted to it by the Supreme Pontiffs: to support the Mother Church of Jerusalem and, in doing so, to take on those initiatives that help the social, educational, and relational coexistence without distinction of gender and in an inclusive vision that favors dialogue between Christian churches and with Jews and Muslims. Since membership in the Order is not bequeathed through dynastic inheritance or privilege or by census, but through "attraction" and "adherence" to its spiritual, moral, and institutional principles, each Member is required to have an adequate period of preparation, which ends with the awarding of the insignia and

----

analogy, our Order could be called "our great parish," in reality, we are inserted into the local churches of which we are natural members, interlocutors, and active collaborators. Consequently, Dames and Knights cannot alienate themselves from them; the care of relations with the parish and the diocese is of great importance in order to collaborate with them, testify to our belonging there, and make the Order and its purposes known. Laypeople and ecclesiastics, therefore, remain devoted children of their local churches and part of the parishes to which they belong.

special symbols in the Vigil of Arms and Prayer and in the Rite of Investiture.[42]

Sentire cum Ecclesia—which means having a sense of ecclesial communion; thinking, speaking, and acting in order to make the Church grow in depth and extension in fidelity to the Risen Christ—will always be the guiding principle for a Dame and a Knight of the Order of the Holy Sepulchre of Jerusalem. Jesus' words on this are clear: "He who does not gather with me scatters";[43] the temptations of division, of envy, of jealousy, of excelling, are evils crouching at the door of our existence. The Lord has warned us of them. But the works of charity, and above all the holiness of the Members, their testimony of missionary spirit and unity, allow us to overcome the difficulties and live in adherence to the Spirit of the Risen Jesus. Faith is exercised in this, and faith gives us God, and also [gives us] to God.

In the ecclesiological-spiritual context, the Grand Master and the ecclesiastical Members help

[42] The 2020 Constitution in article 35 provides for, in addition to admissions, also resignation, and in article 39 deals with disciplinary measures.

[43] Luke 11:23.

the Order to be in harmony with the Universal Church, with the local churches to which they belong, and with the Church of Jerusalem. These are essential relationships, that we might always remember "who we are" and our "situation" and our "mission" in the context of the framework of adherence to the Pontifical Magisterium. Belonging to the Order leads us to keep our gaze constantly fixed on the Church and on Our Lord pierced[44] and glorified by the Father.[45]

St. Leo the Great wrote that "he who truly wants to honor the Passion of the Lord must look with the eyes of the heart on the Crucified Jesus, in order to recognize his own flesh in his holiness."[46] And the bishop St. Basil commented: "The sufferings, the Cross, the burial, [and] the Resurrection are for the salvation of man so that he may again, through the imitation of Christ, claim his adoption as son, which he was

---

[44] See John 19:37; Zech. 12:10.

[45] See John 12:28.

[46] St. Leo the Great, *Discorsi* (no. 15) *sulla passione del Signore*, cfr. 3–4, *PL* 54, pp. 3566–3567. Translated from the Italian.

endowed with from the beginning."[47] For authenticity of the Christian life and fidelity to spirituality, it is necessary, always and constantly, for Members of the Order of the Holy Sepulchre of Jerusalem to conform to the mystery of Jesus and the Church, mindful of the teaching of the Lord: "If any man would come after me ... take up his cross and follow me."[48]

If "communion" *ad intra* [within] in the Church is one of the constitutive principles for an authentic spirituality, such as "People of God" and "Body of Christ," no less so is that *ad extra* [outside] that tends to overcome divisions with realities other than the Catholic Church, present in the Holy Land and elsewhere. I think of the numerous confessions, Christian and non-Christian, who need for there to be dialogue, mutual knowledge, esteem, and respect, excluding all forms of scandalous hostility or dominance.

An evangelical passage comes to our aid, one in which the disciple in Gethsemane, intending to defend the Lord against those who have come to take

[47] St. Basil the Great, *Libro "Su lo Spirito Santo"* 15; PG 32, 127. Translated from the Italian.
[48] Matt. 16:24; Mark 8:34; Luke 9:23.

Him "with swords and clubs," resorts to the "sword" himself.[49] Jesus not only asks [him] to put the sword away, but, in fact, refers to the teaching elsewhere proclaimed: " Unless your righteousness exceeds that of the scribes and Pharisees, you will never enter the kingdom of heaven."[50] And again: "You have heard that it was said, 'An eye for an eye and a tooth for a tooth.' But I say to you, Do not resist one who is evil."[51] Those who intend to follow Christ will then have to respond to evil with nonviolence, implementing dialogue and reason, because with those words,

---

[49] Matt. 26:51, 55; Mark 14:42; Luke 22:43; John 18:10–11. The Fathers of the Second Vatican Council also expressed their appreciation for those who did not use violence in defense of their own rights: "We cannot fail to praise those who renounce the use of violence in the vindication of their rights and who resort to methods of defense which are otherwise available to weaker parties too." Pastoral Constitution on the Church in the Modern World *Gaudium et Spes* (December 7, 1965), no. 78. Forgiveness — including that of the enemy — mercy, and reconciliation are the highest expression of the teaching of Jesus, which we clearly find in chapter 5 of the Gospel of Matthew (the Sermon on the Mount).

[50] Matt. 5:20.

[51] Matt. 5:38–39.

the Lord has changed the relationships dominated by brutality, in order to privilege ethical behavior, which certainly ennobles every man and woman who practices it.

Since the Second Vatican Council, ecumenical dialogue with the Christian Churches has become an irrevocable step. It was desired in various epochs and [in various] ways and became an integral part of the life of the Catholic Church with the Council's decree *Unitatis Redintegratio.*[52] At the same time, with the declaration *Nostra Aetate*, the Council also felt it a duty to promote relations with non-Christian religions, and in particular with Jews and Muslims, since all men are created in the image of God. Concerning the Jews, then, the Council underlined the close bond of the Christians with the lineage of Abraham, to which belong Christ "according to the flesh";[53] Mary, the Mother of Jesus; the apostles and the early Church, while it decried "hatred, persecutions, [and]

[52] Paul VI approved the decree on November 21, 1964; the introduction says: "The restoration of unity among all Christians is one of the principal concerns of the Second Vatican Council."

[53] Rom. 9:5.

displays of anti-Semitism, directed against Jews at any time and by anyone."[54] Concerning Islam, the Council found that "the Church regards with esteem also the Moslems. They adore the one God, living and subsisting in Himself; merciful and all-powerful, the Creator of heaven and earth, who has spoken to men." [The Council] urged "all to forget the past and to work sincerely for mutual understanding and to preserve as well as to promote together, for the benefit of all mankind, social justice and moral welfare, as well as peace and freedom."[55]

The Abu Dhabi *Document on Human Fraternity for World Peace and Living Together* (February 4, 2019) moved in that line.[56] We can therefore believe that

---

[54] Declaration on the Relation of the Church with Non-Christian Religions *Nostra Aetate* (*NA*) (October 28, 1965), no. 4. On this, see also the thought of Pope Francis, who underlines the shared faith in the One God, Who acts in history and whose revelation we welcome in the revealed Word. See Apostolic Exhortation *Evangelii Gaudium* (*EG*) (November 24, 2013), nos. 247–249.

[55] *NA*, no. 3.

[56] The document develops the countless initiatives and pronouncements of St. Paul VI, St. John Paul II, Benedict XVI, and Francis, but it is also an expression of the

the Order of the Holy Sepulchre is placed in the same vein, in a convinced and positive way, also taking into account what Pope Francis has recognized in our Order:

It is a good sign that your initiatives in the field of training and health care are open to all, regardless of the communities they belong to and the religion they profess. In this way you help

thought of various Muslim leaders, such as the Grand Imam of Al-Azhar, Ahmad al-Tayyeb, the co-signer; furthermore, more and more Muslim personalities, Sunni and Shia, converge on this line; for example: Muhammad Bin Abdul Karim al-Issa (Sunni), Mohammad Ali Shomali (Shia) and theologian Shahrzad Houshmand Zadeh (Shia). The vision of relations with Islam was expressed by Pope Francis in *EG*, nos. 252–253. We must overcome the temptation induced by extremist currents and atrocious facts that Christianity and Islam are at war with each other; the diversity of beliefs does not affect those values such as human dignity, peace, mutual respect and human fraternity. War and violence can never be solutions. Please also read the interview that appeared in the *Jerusalem Cross*, 2019–2020 of CardInal M. A. Ayuso Guixot on the reasons that led to the agreement and signature of this historic document. On fraternity, it is not possible to ignore the encyclical *Fratelli Tutti* by Pope Francis.

pave the way to make Christian values known, to the promotion of interreligious dialogue, mutual respect and mutual understanding. In other words, with your commendable commitment, you too offer your contribution to build the path that will lead ... to the achievement of peace throughout the region.[57]

The Magisterium of the Church and the Order

In the context of the ecclesiological dimension, at this point it would be beneficial briefly to recall the most recent [teachings of the] Magisterium of the Church with regard to the Equestrian Order of the Holy Sepulchre of Jerusalem. It is an important aspect because the thought of the Supreme Pontiffs appears in all its clarity.

Approving the updating of the Constitution of the Order in 1962, John XXIII wrote:

Naturally, similar to other institutions that are well organized and of proper vitality, this family

---

[57] Francis, *Address to Members of the Consulta.*

of Knights must clearly understand how those
who direct it, under the guidance of the Cardinal
Grand Master, must try, with all their strength, to
achieve the noblest and highest fidelity assigned
to the Order: that is to say that Members increasingly feed their souls in the Christian spirit,
defend and spread the Faith in the homeland of
the Divine Redeemer and inflame men to love
the Savior.[58]

In turn, in 1964 Paul VI said:

An institution like yours attracts the public's
gaze and esteem for the two aspects it clearly
represents: the exterior, your uniforms, your
insignia, your meetings; and the inner one,
of your adhesion to the Faith and to Catholic
life, indeed to the militia and service of the
Church and the cause of Jesus Christ, especially
in those Holy Places that were the humble and
incomparable scene of the Gospel and are still

[58] John XXIII, Apostolic Brief *Religiosissimo a Monu-
mento Victoriae* (December 8, 1962), in *AAS* (1963),
pp. 444–446. Translated from the Italian.

the framework of facts and religious interests, to which the Holy See, and with it the whole Catholic world, always attach utmost importance. Therefore, one rule can be said to govern your own institution: correspondence, coherence, the mutual reflection of one aspect in the other. What use would the external signs of your Order be if they were not indicative of a sincere and lived profession of Catholic faith, both within the hearts and moral style that should mark the life of a Knight of the Holy Sepulchre? Are these insignia that declare your adherence to an elected and qualified militia of Christ not symbols, stimuli, bonds of your fidelity to his cause, of your exemplarity in the society in which you find yourself, of your rejection of inertia, passivity, fatigue in favor of active, generous, militant adhesion to the Holy Church? This is what it wants to be; this is how your belonging to the Order of the Holy Sepulchre should be.

May your spirits be pervaded by this invigorating awareness, that you have truly realized in yourself the honor of belonging to it, and, by doing so, you also give the Order itself the best confirmation of its reason for existing, its vigorous fullness of discipline and activity, its highest level of merit and glory.... Continue to love those Holy Places, with an increasingly intense and pious predilection; continue to seek and honor the land sanctified by the steps of the Son of God, Who became Son of man; continue to promote there the works of religion, education, and charity that attest to the tenacious and loving presence of the Catholic Church; if possible, increase your effort of spiritual and corporal beneficence for those populations.[59]

After these memorable words, we now ponder those of the Popes closest to us and whom we remember with respect and affection. In 2000, on the occasion of the Holy Year, John Paul II expressed himself in the following terms to the participants in the Order's Jubilee:

[59] Paul VI, Address to the Equestrian Order of the Holy Sepulchre (May 30, 1964), in *AAS* 56, pp. 572–574. Translated from the Italian.

There is an ancient and glorious bond between your chivalrous confraternity and the place of Christ's Sepulchre, where the glory of the Resurrection is celebrated in a most particular way. This is the very focal point of your spirituality. To renew this millenary bond and to make your Gospel witness ever more living and eloquent, you have written new guidelines for your work within the framework of your order's Statutes. You know, in fact, that the beginning of a new millennium demands an updated interpretation of the rule of life for your particular service. For you, as for every Christian, a fresh appreciation of Baptism, the basis of all Christian life, is crucial. This requires careful reflection on the *Catechism* and the Bible, a serious review of life and generous apostolic zeal. Thus you will be open to today's world without losing the spirit of the order, whose desired renewal depends above all on the personal conversion of each individual. As your motto says: "*Oportet gloriari in Cruce Domini Nostri Iesu Christi*": we must glory in the Cross of Our Lord Jesus Christ. Let Christ be the heart of your life, of your every project and programme, both as individuals and as an association.[60]

These concepts would subsequently be reaffirmed by Pope Benedict XVI in 2008, when he addressed these heartfelt words to the Members of the Consulta of the Order:

What need the Land of Jesus has for justice and peace! Continue to work for this and do not tire in asking, with the Prayer of the Knights and the Ladies of the Holy Sepulchre, that as soon as possible these aspirations may come to completion. Ask the Lord to make you "convinced and sincere ambassadors of peace and love among your brethren," ask him to make fruitful, with the power of his love, your constant work to support the ardent desire for peace in those communities weighed down by a climate of uncertainty and danger in the last years....

May the Virgin of Nazareth ... assist you in your mission of watching over with love upon

[60] John Paul II Address to the Equestrian Order of the Holy Sepulchre (March 2, 2000), no. 3.

the places that saw the Divine Redeemer pass "doing good works and healing all who were in the grip of the devil, for God was with him" (Acts 10:38).[61]

Finally, Pope Francis, urging participants in the Order's pilgrimage in 2013, recalled, "Journey in order to build a community, above all with love." He added:

The Equestrian Order of the Holy Sepulchre of Jerusalem has an almost thousand-year history: yours is one of the oldest charitable Orders that is still active. Established by the Custody of the Holy Sepulchre, it has enjoyed the special attention of the Bishop of Rome. To build with charity, with compassion, with love.... However your journey to build is born of confessing in an ever deeper way the faith; it grows from continued commitment to nourish your spiritual life, from permanent formation to an ever more authentic and consistent Christian

[61] Benedict XVI, Address to the Members of the Equestrian Order of the Holy Sepulchre of Jerusalem (December 5, 2008).

life. This is an important point for each one of you and for the Order as a whole, so that each person is helped to deepen his adherence to Christ: the profession of faith and the testimony of charity are closely connected and are the strong key points that qualify your action. An ancient bond ties you to the Holy Sepulchre, the perennial memorial of Christ Crucified who was laid there and of the Risen Christ who conquered death.... To believe in the redemptive power of the Cross and the Resurrection to offer hope and peace. In a special way, the Land of Jesus needs it very much! The faith does not distance us from the responsibilities that we are all called to assume, but, on the contrary, it urges and impels us to concrete undertakings for a better society.[62]

The special ties with the Holy Land, and in particular with the City of David and the Holy Sepulchre, referred to in the papal teaching, remind us, once

---

[62] Francis, Address to the Participants in the Pilgrimage of the Equestrian Order of the Holy Sepulchre of Jerusalem, (September 13, 2013), nos. 2–3.

again, of how much they require our affection and our generous response, being places where the Lord spent His earthly life, where His Word was heard, and where He offered His life, establishing in His person a New Covenant between God and man. It is a Covenant that transcends the old one and that has definitively opened the "election" once reserved for Israel to the inclusion of the "pagans," according to the clear teaching of the apostle Paul in the Letter to the Romans (chapter 11). The offering of Jesus to the Father, in fact, had become indispensable from the moment in which humanity experienced the departure from its Creator, and, with Cain, there had been the first spilling of fratricidal blood, a shedding that, from then on, has continued to stain the earth. For this reason, the exhortation that John Paul II addressed to the Consulta of the Order in 2003 is precious:

Be builders of love and peace, inspired in your life and actions by the Gospel and especially by the mystery of the passion and Resurrection of Christ. May you take as your model Mary, Mother of Believers and ever-ready to adhere joyfully to God's will. Call upon her every day with the beautiful, traditional prayer of the Rosary that helps us to contemplate Christ with the gaze of his holy Mother. This will be a source of growth for you, as it was for your illustrious confrere, Bl. Bartolo Longo.[63]

Her Name Was Mary

Mary was a very common name in Palestine. Among her young friends [the Mother of Jesus] was known as "Mary of Nazareth," the "kinswoman" of Elizabeth of the tribe of Levi,[64] who was tied to Joseph in affection as his "betrothed."[65] The evangelists Matthew and Luke then speak of the two in relation to conception,

[63] John Paul II, Message to the Consulta of the Equestrian Order of the Holy Sepulchre of Jerusalem (October 16, 2003), no. 3.

[64] See Luke 1:36.

[65] Matt. 1:18; Luke 1:27. The Davidic lineage and the promises made by God to Abraham come to Jesus from the descendants not of Mary, but of Joseph, a Jew, originally from Bethlehem. According to Jewish tradition, it is from the father that this inheritance passes. Thus, Jesus obtains the human-divine nature from Mary (*Theotókos*, see CCC 466) and the biblical promises from Joseph.

birth, the prescriptions of the Jewish law regarding firstborn children,[66] and the pilgrimages that the small family made to Jerusalem. In particular, Luke reflects on the pilgrimage to Jerusalem for Passover when the adolescent Jesus was twelve.[67] In Nazareth, Jesus was known as the son of the carpenter and of Mary: "Is not this the carpenter's son? Is not his mother called Mary?"[68]

Mary rarely appears in the public life of the Lord. She remains in the background. John says she is still present at the marriage feast in Cana in Galilee, where she is referred to as "the mother of Jesus";[69] Mark, on another occasion, mentions her as "his [Jesus'] mother ... [when his brethren] called him." Jesus was teaching, and He seemed almost to withdraw from the blood relationship to establish a new one: "Whoever does the will of God is my brother, and sister, and mother."[70] Already in Cana in Galilee, addressing His mother with the term "woman" rather than "mother" ("Jesus replied:

[66] See Luke 2:21–39.
[67] See Luke 2:41–50.
[68] Matt. 13:55; Mark 6:3.
[69] John 2:1.
[70] Mark 3:31–35.

"Woman, what have you to do with me?").[71] And then on the Cross ("He said to his mother: 'Woman, behold your son!'"), Jesus seems to conclude his temporal relationship with Mary to pass it on to John ("Then he said to the disciple: 'Behold your mother!'") and, through him, to the new family that was being formed with His death ("And from that hour the disciple took her to his own home").[72]

Indeed, from then on, Mary will belong to the Church. From the height of the Cross, therefore, Jesus defines Mary's new motherhood by placing her forever in the Church. Thus, we find "Mary the mother of Jesus,"[73] present in the apostolic community, persevering in prayer on the day of Pentecost. The two Gospel passages mentioned above, the event at the foot of the Cross and the one relating to the presence of Mary among the apostles at Pentecost, belong to the most significant and dearest moments of the Catholic Marian tradition. Mary entered into a new family, formed with Christ's death and Resurrection,

[71] John 2:4.
[72] John 19:26–27.
[73] Acts 1:14. It is the last mention of Mary's name and role in the New Testament.

and from then on, she will belong to the community of believers. In this capacity—in addition to the Christological role connected to her divine motherhood, as the first educator of her Son together with Joseph, and to her discreet but effective presence during His public life—she also assumes a high ecclesial function connected to her femininity, which somehow balances the masculinity constituted by the apostles. Here we like to quote a significant and illuminating expression of Benedict XVI, who writes that "the Church's juridical structure is founded on Peter and the Eleven, but in the day-to-day life of the Church, it is the women who are constantly opening the door to the Lord and accompanying him to the Cross, and so it is they who come to experience the Risen One."[74] In truth, the reception of grace in the world had taken place through Mary.

Thus, it is then convenient to pause again, albeit briefly, on the magnificent, elevated, and final human gesture of the dying Jesus' entrusting His mother—the one who had generated, cared for, and accompanied Him everywhere with deep affection—to John. In

[74] Ratzinger, *Jesus of Nazareth*, p. 292.

the Semitic tradition, up to the present day, it is not good for a woman to live alone, also because of the necessities of life. Consequently, it is obvious that she be taken into the care of her child or by a close and trusted relative; in this concrete case, Jesus entrusts His mother to John. Note that this was the last human concern of the Lord. He can now put everything back into the hands of the Father and die having accomplished everything, absolutely everything, even the entrustment of Mary to a trusted person so that she would not remain alone and would have someone to care for her as a new son. It was that gesture that defined Mary's new motherhood in an ecclesiological sense.

The Gospels note her presence next to the Cross, yet they do not speak to us of her immense pain. We can imagine, however, her dignity in faith and her immeasurable suffering of heart. Neither is anything mentioned about the pain that this sorrowful Mother endured during the three days during which her Son lay buried, nor of the immense joy of seeing Him risen. Mary's faith was rising at all times, to reappear in the context of the apostolic community in prayer, awaiting the Holy Spirit. Paul VI glimpsed in all this, with clarity, the maternal role of Mary, proclaiming her "Mother of the Church" at the end of the third session of the Second Vatican Council.[75]

For the Order of the Holy Sepulchre, Mary, with the title Our Lady Queen of Palestine[76] —an attribution established perpetually by Pope John Paul II on January 21, 1994, with the Apostolic Letter *Est*

---

[75] "Therefore to the glory of the Blessed Virgin and to our consolation we declare Mary Most Holy Mother of the Church, that is, of all the Christian people, both of the faithful and of the Shepherds, who call her very beloved Mother; and we establish that with this title all the Christian people from now on pay even more honor to the Mother of God and make supplications to her." Allocution of November 21, 1964, in *AAS* 56 (1964), pp. 1007–1018. Translated from the Italian. On February 11, 2018, Pope Francis established her liturgical feast on the Monday after Pentecost.

[76] For the first time the title Queen of Palestine was used by the Latin Patriarch of Jerusalem Luigi Barlassina in 1920, then formally attributed by the Congregation of Rites in 1933; as for the image, there are several: from the one venerated at Deir Rafat, where Barlassina erected a sanctuary in 1927, to the more recent ones that are preserved in some Lieutenancies. See the art of G. Motta, in AD 2012 (The Past Year 2011), pp. 33–37.

Quidem[77] — is liturgically venerated as Patron on October 25.

Therefore, there are profound reasons for the Order's particular heartfelt love for the Mother of Jesus, to whom we turn as a beacon of peaceful coexistence between Christians and the peoples who inhabit the Holy Land, a land blessed by the very historical presence of Mary, where she has not yet fully exhausted the special mission entrusted to her by Providence.

> *"Then he led them out as far as Bethany,*
> *and lifting up his hands he blessed them."*[78]

The gesture of blessing concludes the Risen Christ's mission among us. It is a protective and farewell gesture; it is not a goodbye. Jesus "returns" to the Father and to the Trinitarian communion as true God,

---

[77] With the Decree of the Congregation for Divine Worship and the Discipline of the Sacraments, *Est Quidem: Beata Maria Virgo Titulo "Domina Nostra Palestinae Regina"* (January 25, 2019), the inscription in the General Roman Calendar of the celebration already foreseen by Pope Paul VI took place.

[78] Luke 24:50.

bringing with Him all human experience, as true man. This is not a secondary aspect. This "bringing" His humanity means that, although now glorious, Jesus renounces nothing of what He has lived. After all, we could say, in an analogical sense: God "is enriched" with it. He brings His face to the Father, with the request for forgiveness, with His generation according to the flesh, with His human and religious education, with His awareness of life spent in a family, with His faith lived in the Jewish tradition, with the most varied human relationships: feelings in relation to a mother, father, friends, fellow villagers, relatives, women, enemies, Romans, accusers, beneficiaries, Pharisees, priests of the Temple, apostles. He brings with Him the experience of sharing in people's lives: of being moved at the death of his friend Lazarus and for the son of Nain's widow, solidarity with lepers, the struggle to free the tormented from the devil; and more still: the sensation of hunger, temptation, betrayal, anguish, fear, the closure of hearts and minds toward Him. He also brings with Him, and forever, the joy in praying that fascinated the disciples, the intimate joy for those who enjoyed forgiveness, the fervor of the people satiated by bread, the irrepressible happiness of those who had been cured of socially excluding infirmities, the gratitude of the poor, amazement at nature: His gaze at the birds of the sky, His observation of the lilies of the field.[79] In short, every aspect of his existence spent among us. But above all, He carries in His mind the sensation of pain experienced in His body: an unjust condemnation, the deepest humiliation, abandonment, and that physical torment from wounds that never healed, through which He will always implore for us the Father's understanding. Finally, death. He left to us the teaching of someone who has authority: love your enemies and pray for your persecutors.[80]

With the Ascension, therefore, Jesus concludes His historical experience, geographically located in and around Palestine. He does not go somewhere but inaugurates a new relationship with us, according to His own words: "And lo, I am with you always, to the close of the age";[81] and He promises, "You shall receive power when the Holy Spirit has come upon you."[82]

[79] See Matt. 6:26–28.
[80] See Matt. 5:44.
[81] Matt. 28:20.
[82] Acts 1:8.

From now on, He will be another, new presence; in fact, St. Paul teaches that we no longer know Him according to the flesh,[83] but according to faith and baptismal grace.

The Church now lives in the light of this promise and faith in carrying out the mission of teaching all peoples, baptizing them for their incorporation into the Trinitarian life of grace left to them as an incomparable gift from Jesus. Contributing to this mission is the greatest honor that the Lord gives us, which opens us to joy, when our names are written in heaven.[84]

---

[83] See 2 Cor. 5:16.
[84] See Luke 10:20.

About the Author

Cardinal Fernando Filoni was born on April 15, 1946, in Manduria, near Taranto, Italy, and was ordained a priest on July 3, 1970, for the diocese of Nardò (Lecce). He studied in Rome at the Pontifical Lateran University, where he earned a degree in canon law; the Sapienza University, where he earned a degree in philosophy; and the Pro Deo (today the Free International University of Social Studies [LUISS]), where he obtained a postgraduate diploma in Sciences and Techniques of Public Opinion, specializing in journalism. During this period in Rome, he was a parochial vicar, focusing on the education of the young.

He entered the diplomatic service of the Holy See and served in Sri Lanka (1981); he was successively sent to Iran (1983–1985) before being called to the Secretariat of State. He was transferred to Brazil (1989–1992) and then to Hong Kong at a study mission for the care of the Church in China (1992–2001) after the first political opening introduced by Deng Xiaoping in that country. On January 17, 2001, he was appointed titular archbishop of Volturnum and apostolic nuncio to Jordan and Iraq. He received episcopal consecration from Pope John Paul II on March 19, 2001, in the Vatican Basilica.

After Baghdad (2001–2006), Benedict XVI at first appointed him papal representative to the Philippines (2006–2007) and then substitute (deputy) for general affairs of the Secretariat of State.

On May 10, 2011, the same pontiff named him prefect of the Congregation for the Evangelization of Peoples, creating him a cardinal on February 18, 2012.

On December 8, 2019, Pope Francis named him Grand Master of the Equestrian Order of the Holy Sepulchre of Jerusalem and prefect emeritus of the Congregation for the Evangelization of Peoples.

Cardinal Filoni is the author of various writings, including *The Church in Iraq*, which has been translated into different languages.

He is a member of various Congregations in the Roman Curia.